The Stubby

Andrew Mackey lives in Sussex and has a long-standing
interest in health and fitness. He began to investigate
the subject of smoking while watching several close
friends struggling to quit the habit and discovered that
many important facts pertinent to the smoker were
largely unknown. From this awareness,
The Stubby was born.

THE STUBBY
FREEDOM FROM CIGARETTES

Andrew Mackey

Kyle Cathie Limited

First published in Great Britain in 2000 by
Kyle Cathie Limited
122 Arlington Road
London NW1 7HP

ISBN 1 85626 381 9

A Cataloguing in Publication record for this title is available from the
British Library.

Printed and bound in Great Britain by
Cox & Wyman Ltd, Reading, Berkshire

Dedicated to Joanne

Welcome to the Stubby

There is no investment so rewarding as an investment in your health. Your health is the foundation of every act and moment of your life. It can hold you back and make each step painful and slow, or it can carry you forward, allowing you to embrace life to the full. Good health is the vehicle that allows you to take all the world has to offer in your stride. In fact your health *is* your life. To stop smoking is the most important action you can take to improve every aspect of your health and, consequently, your life.

You are not alone in wanting to stop smoking. 70% of all smokers want to quit. Millions already have, and that means that *you* can stop too. There is no bigger aid in the battle to quit smoking than the *will* to stop. Everyone knows they should, but to quit for good, you really have to want to. This book will help you want to. Most people can gather the willpower to stop for a few days or even weeks, but then the resolve may fade. You may feel bored or stressed, or have a strong urge for 'just one' cigarette, and temptation can creep in. You will need to remind yourself why you want to stop. You will need to rebuild your willpower from time to time.

This is where *The Stubby* will help. It reminds you *why* you want to stop smoking and tells you of the dangers that the habit brings. *The Stubby* is packed with shocking yet little known facts that will help to keep you free from cigarettes for good, and it responds to each fact by offering positive suggestions, help and advice. *The Stubby* will be your companion, friend and guide, along the road to freedom. When you feel the urge for your cigarettes, reach for *The Stubby* instead. It will strengthen your will to stop. It will keep you determined to stop.

In the Good News sections towards the back of the book you will find a list of all the improvements to your body and to your life that come along with each day of cigarette freedom. The Help section offers you a list of agencies that exist solely to provide you with further assistance, guidance and support, should you need it.

I hope that you enjoy *The Stubby* and allow it to lead you along the path to greater health and positive living. I hope it will help to free and protect you from the physical and financial damage that is caused by smoking.

ANDREW MACKEY
JANUARY 2000

Each cigarette contains a mixture of 4000 chemicals. These chemicals cause over 50 separate diseases. 24 of them can kill you.

Educate yourself to the facts of smoking. Take a step back and think about your habit. Consider the impact that smoking will ultimately have on your body. Try to think of just one positive result of smoking. Ask yourself why you smoke.

Non-smokers who have been inhaling other people's tobacco smoke for most of their lives have a 10–30% higher risk of developing lung cancer.

With the money you save from not smoking, treat yourself to some new plants to place around the house. Houseplants clean the air and give out oxygen. Revitalise your workplace and home. Having plants around will help you feel calmer and more relaxed.

It is estimated that around 50 children under 5 years old are admitted to hospital every day, suffering from illnesses brought about by passive smoking.

You can really turn things around to benefit your children. Why not consider spending some of the money you save from not smoking on family membership of a local sports club? Decide to be a healthier family.

80% of heart attacks in men under 45 are thought to have been caused by smoking.

There are mountains to be climbed, hills to be walked, fish to be landed, rare birds to be seen. There are many more interesting things to look forward to than another cigarette. Think about how you can widen your view of life.

Smoking is known to speed up the appearance of wrinkles. A woman who has always smoked 20 cigarettes a day can expect by the age of 35 to have the complexion of a 45-year-old.

Given the choice, most people would prefer to appear young and healthy. Many people spend a large amount of money trying to keep their skin looking youthful. By not smoking you will have visibly healthier skin. The difference will be seen in your mirror.

Smoking increases a man's chances of impotence by 50%. Smoking thickens blood, making it less able to fill the small blood vessels of the penis, and therefore reduces penis size and strength.

Consider the importance of a happy and healthy sex life. By not smoking you will avoid many intimate problems that smoking can bring. Do not think of giving up cigarettes as losing something from your life. Rather, realise that by not smoking you will be gaining many positive benefits and improvements.

10,000 people die every month because they smoked. Over 300 people every day. That's equal to a jumbo jet crashing to the ground every 24 hours.

Why not decide to live life as fully as you can? You will not only feel better physically for not smoking, you will also feel better personally because you will have proven to yourself (and everyone else) that you can quit. You'll also feel much better financially because you'll have more money to spend, on whatever you choose.

A person who smokes is 2–3 times more likely to have a heart attack than a non-smoker.

You may feel the need to do something with your hands when you first stop smoking. Why not try drawing or painting? It does not have to be clever or serious, just enjoy yourself. Even simply colouring in a child's book can be therapeutic and satisfying.

**Smoking doubles the
chances of developing
Alzheimer's disease.**

No matter how long you have been smoking it is definitely never too late to stop. Pick a date to quit well in advance, so when that day arrives, your subconscious will already be prepared. You will have pre-programmed yourself by turning the date for quitting over and over in your mind.

Studies which examined the saliva in children's mouths found that in a home where both parents regularly smoke, a child receives the equivalent of 80 cigarettes a year.

The single greatest thing that you can do for your own health is to stop smoking. The single greatest thing you can do for your children's health is the same. Stop smoking as a gesture of love for your family. Protect your children.

Smoking inevitably makes your hair, your breath and your clothes smell.

Professionally and personally, by not smoking, you'll make a far better impression. You will no longer need to worry whether the first thing people notice about you is the smell of cigarette smoke. Your entire appearance will be healthier, brighter and fresher. This can only bring rewards.

Smokers' arteries thicken 50% faster than those of non-smokers.

Investigate and realise the risks of smoking. Carry this book with you and any time you feel the urge to smoke, open it to remind yourself why you want to quit. Make a small ritual of declaring yourself free from cigarettes. Throw away all smoking equipment, and write down why you are giving up smoking.

Smoking 40 cigarettes a day costs over £2700 per year.

Imagine if you had to pay for a year's supply of cigarettes in advance. Would you really hand over thousands of pounds simply to inhale smoke for the next 12 months? Or do you think you could find a better use for the money?

Cigarette smoke contains a radioactive element called polonium 210. It has been estimated that smoking 20 cigarettes a day is the equivalent of receiving 200 chest X-rays each year.

Find out what smoking really does to you. Be better informed. Would you feel happy about having 200 X-rays every year? Remember, that's the comparison with only a 20-cigarette-per-day smoker.

Smokers are twice as likely as non-smokers to suffer hearing loss.

I'm sure you enjoy music and conversation. The singing of birds in your garden? Why risk the pleasure of those things for the sake of a cigarette? Treat yourself to some new music to remind yourself that not smoking brings many rewards and avoids many problems.

The danger that an average smoker places on the heart is the same as someone who does not smoke increasing his or her weight by 10 stone.

Picture yourself in your mind's eye or stand before your mirror. Now add 10 extra stone of body weight. How do you look? This is the added strain placed on your heart from smoking. Repeat this visualisation when you feel the urge for a cigarette.

Children of smokers are 2–3 times more likely to smoke. In effect, they start smoking from the moment of birth, by passively sharing their parents' cigarettes.

Most people would fight to the end to protect the lives of their children. If your child needed a blood transfusion you would roll up your sleeve in a split second. Surely if you can protect their health by not smoking, you will stop.

Government regulations do not allow industrial workers to be exposed to carbon monoxide levels above 50 parts per million. Tobacco smoke can contain carbon monoxide at levels of between 1000 and 50,000 parts per million.

Would you be happy to work in an environment that was most certainly going to destroy your health? It may seem obvious, but do we truly realise that the body we have now is the only one we will ever have? Do not allow yours to be poisoned for other people's profit.

Stress breaks down the levels of nicotine in the body, and so leads to cravings for a cigarette. Cigarettes do not help you to relax; they only highlight your body's addiction to the presence of nicotine.

Try meditation – there will be classes near you. Learn to be calm in life. You can rise above anything. Practise putting things into perspective. Think about how important any current problem will seem, just one year from now.

**In the UK, 120,000 people die
each year from smoking.**

Decide to embrace your life. Be positive and choose to live to your fullest potential. If giving up for good seems too daunting, try giving up for one year, or just one month. You may find that you can repeat a less intimidating goal indefinitely. The first few weeks are usually the hardest. Aim to beat them.

Smoking during pregnancy can lead to smaller, underdeveloped babies and increases the risk of birth defects. Lead, cadmium and nicotine can all be found in the breast milk of mothers who smoke.

Children are the strongest bond in life. Parents would do anything to avoid them suffering. You can help your children from the very start by simply being a non-smoking parent.

The carbon monoxide from cigarette smoke poisons the muscles of the heart. Smokers have double the risk of coronary heart disease.

Take up exercise and double up
on the benefits of not smoking.
Oxygen will nourish your heart
and exercise will strengthen it.
Look after your heart.

Cancers linked to smoking include cancer of the mouth, throat, bladder, pancreas, cervix and penis.

Unfortunately many smokers hear of the danger of smoking only from the companies who sell cigarettes. No wonder the true dangers are little known. Smoking affects the entire body in a negative way. It is often said, but life is for living. Your body is the foundation of the life you lead and smoking will destroy it.

Children who grow up in a smoke-filled home are twice as likely to develop asthma. They are also much more likely to suffer from pneumonia and bronchitis.

If you smoke, your family does too. This may sound obvious, but it is often not truly realised. Be a non-smoker for the sake of your children. You can view this gesture as free life insurance for them. They will be healthier if you do not smoke.

Carbon monoxide found in cigarette smoke is also emitted by car exhausts. The carbon monoxide from car exhausts is often used as a means of committing suicide.

Think of your cigarette as a car exhaust. Are you sure that you enjoy breathing that smoke? Choose to be free from the pretty boxes and clever marketing of poison.

The average weight gain from giving up smoking is only 4 lb. This is usually temporary and often there is no increase at all. In fact, 20% of ex-smokers say they lost weight when they stopped.

It is not true that smoking keeps you slim. Do not let petty excuses stop you from being free from the smoking habit. There is no positive argument in favour of smoking.

One out of four smokers who starts in his or her teens will lose around 25 years of life.

Study books on health and well-being, cultivate an interest in what you eat and what you do. See what small changes you can make to your life to reap big rewards.

Of all continual smokers only 10% survive to the age of 75. Most non-smokers can reach 75 in good health.

Decide to enjoy sharing the lives of your children and your grandchildren. Do not take this thought lightly. The threat is real. Smoking will shorten your life. Resolve to live as long and as happily as you can.

In Britain approximately 12 people die on the roads each day. But 100 die each day from lung cancer, 100 from chronic bronchitis and 100 from heart attacks, all of which are caused mainly by smoking.

The argument of 'you might be

hit by a bus tomorrow' is not

backed up by the statistics.

In developed countries such as the UK one in three men die before age 65, mainly due to smoking.

Too many men work hard for years and save towards their pension but die before spending a single penny of it, because they smoked. Do not let smoking rob you of your retirement or the money that you are saving towards it.

The smoke from tobacco includes traces of cyanide, acetone, hydrogen, ammonia and formaldehyde. More than 50 of the chemicals in cigarette smoke are thought to cause cancer.

Go into a hardware store and look at the bottles of chemicals on the shelf. How many would you happily drink from? Now look at the opposite list again. Care about what you put into your body.

**One in two regular smokers
are killed by their habit
with an average life loss of
16 years.**

Would you really want to risk losing around 16 years of your life just for the sake of smoking? Isn't that just like pouring a large part of your life straight down the drain? If cigarettes were free the cost would still be far too high.

Premature birth is twice as common in smokers. Smoking also accounts for more than 4000 miscarriages every year in England and Wales.

Spend some time in your garden or local park. Rediscover the nature that surrounds you. It is surprising how much amazing life there is around us if we just take the extra few minutes to look. The smallest part of nature can give inspiration and strength.

Three times more smokers than non-smokers die in middle age.

Talk to your doctor or chemist about Nicotine Replacement Therapy (NRT). By allowing your body to receive controlled doses of nicotine, via a patch or gum, etc., you may find it easier to break the habit of smoking. Studies have shown this to be a highly effective technique.

Smokers are much more likely to have regular sleep problems. A smoker gets approximately 30 minutes less sleep each night than a non-smoker.

Sleep is nature's way of repairing and rejuvenating the body. By not smoking you will be able to indulge in more relaxed sleep. Why not splash out on some fresh new bedding and candles for your bedroom? You quit smoking to improve your life. You're saving money. So treat yourself.

Smoking brings the female menopause earlier by an average of two years.

Become an expert in longevity. Find out what supplements, vitamins and exercise can do to extend your life. Realise that you can actually slow down the aging of your body by better living. You can feel younger. You can look younger.

Smoking decreases bone density, increasing the risk of osteoporosis (brittle bone disease), and can cause weakening of the bone around the teeth, making them more likely to fall out.

Join a gym and work your body. Along with your muscles and bones you will also strengthen your resolve. The results of exercise will encourage you not to smoke as you see improvement in the shape and health of your body.

The rate of stillbirths among smokers is about a third higher than in non-smokers. This represents around 420 deaths per year in England and Wales.

Smoking while pregnant is an unnecessary risk. Allow pregnancy to be an incentive to stop smoking for good. What better time could there be to make a healthy decision? Let the prospect of good health be your first gift to your child. There is nothing more valuable.

Smoking ages the skin dramatically. This is more obvious in women because their skin is thinner and the damage shows more easily.

Remember that damage from smoking happens to the outside of your body as well as the inside. Refuse to allow the habit of smoking to age you prematurely. Pamper yourself and enjoy improving your appearance. Have a facial massage and kick-start the improvements to your skin.

**95% of men with lung cancer
are smokers.**

Encourage some friends to get into some form of sport with you. It's an opportunity to be sociable. Being healthy does not have to be hard work. Simply get out there and enjoy yourself.

Smoking can clog the delicate blood vessels in your arms and legs, making smokers more prone to gangrene, which can lead to amputation. Smoking is the biggest cause of more than 2000 amputations every year in England and Wales.

Do not take your mobility for granted. We often underestimate, or even neglect, the pleasure of movement. Take the time to enjoy the places that walking can get you to. The countryside is not just a thing to watch on television. Rediscover the pleasures of simply walking, breathing and looking.

Nicotine is one of the most addictive substances known to man. It is so poisonous it can be used in the garden as an insecticide. Smoking 20 cigarettes a day means that you will be inhaling nicotine about 73,000 times a year.

Think about starting yoga.
There will be courses near you
or books on the subject in your
library. It is extremely
beneficial for everyone. Learn
to breathe effectively and to
relax. Make a decision to
nourish and nurture yourself.

By the time most cases of lung cancer are finally diagnosed, the chances of a cure are only one in 50.

When you have stopped smoking, say that you don't smoke. Avoid saying that you are 'trying to quit'. Trying implies that you think you might fail. Be determined. Be positive.

A baby's risk of cot death is 3–4 times higher if its mother smokes, and 5 times higher if both parents smoke.

The money saved by not smoking could be spent on treats for your children. Why not set a goal each month that will bring happiness to them, such as a special day out, or a family trip to a restaurant? You'll enjoy yourselves and become a closer family.

One minute after starting to smoke, the smoker's heartbeat speeds up by almost 30%. The body reacts as if it were under stress. Smoking also increases blood pressure.

Try to watch a funny movie or a comedy video one night each week. Laughter is a great medicine. Make yourself laugh – it's good for you.

Smoking directly affects the skin's blood supply and decreases the nutrients and oxygen that the skin receives. Smokers are almost 5 times more likely to be heavily lined than non-smokers.

*No one wants to age
prematurely with a heavily
lined face. Wouldn't you prefer
to look young for your years,
and to hear people say, 'Really?
I thought you were younger.'
Not smoking can actually make
that difference.*

Worldwide, one person dies every 10 seconds from smoking. In the UK alone, smoking leads to a death every 5 minutes.

Imagine a national lottery that created a millionaire every 5 minutes. Would you like to be in that draw? Of course you would. You would probably feel there was a good chance of your number coming up. Unfortunately, smokers are in a lottery exactly like that, but the prize is not desirable.

Smoking can alter the effect of medications and drugs. A woman who takes a contraceptive pill and also smokes has a chance of a heart attack or stroke 10 times greater than a woman who does neither.

Have you thought about how pleased you will feel for giving up smoking? The boost to your self-esteem? The relief? Every other smoker will envy you and wish for your resolve. You can do it.

90% of lung cancer and bronchitis deaths are due to smoking.

Think of sports that you used to enjoy and consider taking them up again. You may have enjoyed tennis or squash in the past. The chances are you would enjoy them just as much now. Try, though do remember to take things gently to begin with.

Smoking 60 cigarettes

a day wastes over £4000

every year.

You have probably been spending a lot of money on cigarettes. So why not find out about investments? A person who quits smoking effectively gets a big pay rise, so look at ways to send that money out to work. Start by reading the financial sections in the newspapers.

Smoking is the largest single preventable cause of death.

People who smoke are in the unusual position of being able to stop the most likely cause of their own death. By saying 'no' to smoking you are saying 'yes' to life.

In the USA, 53,000 deaths a year are thought to be due to passive smoking. That's over 1000 people a week who die because other people smoke.

*When you give up cigarettes,
pick up some travel brochures
to remind yourself about your
new freedom. Plan a goal.
Treat yourself to the holiday
of a lifetime with the money
you've saved. Giving up means
getting more.*

Smoking causes a serious threat to those you love. A smoker increases the risk of heart disease affecting their wife, husband or partner by 30%.

Turn your home into a haven from the stresses and strains of the outside world. Choose some new colours and repaint your rooms. You will feel less inclined to smoke in a fresh home. Invest in optimism.

One in every 16 cases of childhood cancers can be linked to passive smoking in the home.

Savings from not smoking for one year would allow the average smoker to purchase a computer system for the home and to extend the family's world outlook via the Internet. A bonus to the family, paid for with money you would previously have burned.

Only one in 12 smoking mothers gives up during pregnancy, and two thirds of those return to smoking after giving birth. If all pregnant mothers were to give up, the number of miscarriages would be halved.

Smoking during pregnancy simply means that the baby shares the cigarette and every danger that comes from it. By being a non-smoker you will be taking a huge step to protect the health of your baby.

In 1990 Perrier withdrew millions of bottles of their spring water because some batches accidentally contained a suspected cancer-promoting substance called benzene at a level of 4.7 micrograms. A single cigarette contains 190 micrograms.

Some facts speak for themselves.
Let's be equally responsible with
our own bodies.

Women who smoke are four times more likely to develop cervical cancer than those who don't.

Smoking attacks even the most intimate parts of our bodies. Women and men will avoid many distressing personal problems by looking after themselves better. Giving up smoking will allow you to indulge yourself more. Try an aromatherapy massage the next time you feel stressed.

Nicotine stimulates the body to produce adrenaline, which makes the heart beat faster. Meanwhile, smoking thickens the blood and narrows the arteries, making it more difficult for blood to be moved around the body.

Make no mistake about the dangers of smoking. Often the first sign of danger is a heart attack or stroke. Give up smoking before your heart gives up for you. The body is an expert at recovery – give it the chance.

91% of all patients considered for a coronary bypass are smokers.

Hospitals are not places in which most of us want to spend time. When you stop smoking, the body starts to improve immediately, and the chances of you needing to visit a hospital decrease sharply. You become fitter, just by quitting.

Because smoking thickens the blood it becomes increasingly difficult for it to enter the finer blood vessels of the skin, turning a once healthy pink face into one that is pale and drawn, resulting in an unattractive sallow complexion.

Adopt a healthy lifestyle. If you cut down on junk food, quit smoking, drink more water and eat more fresh fruit and vegetables, you cannot help but look and feel better.

In the UK, about 450 children start smoking each day. Around a quarter of all British 15-year-olds are regular smokers.

Talk to young people you know and tell them why you gave up smoking. Try to encourage them to lead a healthier life. Be a good example to the young. You will find that discussing things positively will help your own resolve.

People often think twice about inviting smokers to their home purely because they dislike the smell of cigarette smoke and know that it will linger around the house.

It is true that smokers are often unwelcome in public and private places. By being a non-smoker you will have more freedom and be more welcome wherever you go. You will no longer have to ask if it is 'OK' for you to smoke.

49% of all children in the UK are exposed to tobacco smoke at home. In households where both parents smoke, young children have a 72% increased risk of respiratory illness.

Cultivate your garden – it will get you out of the house and into fresh air. You'll find it relaxing as you get back to nature, and it will help to take your mind off smoking.
Why not give your children their own patch and get them to join in?

Tobacco is the only legally available drug that kills people when used exactly as intended.

Be one of the millions who have chosen to reclaim their life and improve their health, by giving up the smoking habit. Some people will certainly profit from you smoking, but you will never be one of them. Smokers can only lose.

Smoking causes cancer of the mouth, lip, throat, stomach, kidney and liver.

As you apply lipstick or shave your face, consider those less fortunate who have had cancer diagnosed on their lip, mouth or throat. Think about how you would feel to be told the same. By not smoking you will dramatically reduce the likelihood of ever having that misfortune.

More than 90% of lung cancer patients die within 5 years of diagnosis.

If you were to be diagnosed with cancer you would almost certainly stop smoking, or wish you had. Why wait? If you stop before you have to, your lungs can recover.

People who smoke over 25 cigarettes a day run a 25 times higher risk of dying from lung cancer than non-smokers.

Replace 25 cigarettes a day with 25 minutes of exercise and see and feel the difference. Start very gently. If one sit-up is more than you do at the moment, then that's a start. Slowly build up. Fitness is not a test. Just do a little every day.

Smoking while pregnant brings an increased risk of spontaneous abortion and haemorrhaging.

Swim during pregnancy. You will find the buoyancy relaxing and you'll increase the oxygen supply to your baby, helping him or her to grow happy and healthy. Of course, even if you are not pregnant, swimming is one of the best forms of exercise you can take. Don't just save it for holidays.

Smoke that drifts from a cigarette is even more toxic than smoke inhaled because it does not pass through a filter. It has been estimated that hundreds of cases of lung cancer occur in British non-smokers every year because of other people smoking.

Why not put the money that you will be saving by not smoking into a Christmas fund? You'll be able to afford to be more generous, so why not give out gifts to all your friends and family? Spread around the positive results of giving up cigarettes.

Around 40% of all heavy smokers die before the age of 65.

Life is already short. Sadly, most people don't realise how wonderful life really is until they are faced with losing it. Don't let smoking rob you of the chance to enjoy a full life. Take time out each day to appreciate your life. Counting your blessings is not a new idea, but it's surprising how high you do count if you try it.

Dentists warn of the dangers of smoking. It affects the colour and stability of teeth as well as potentially leading to cancers of the lip, tongue and mouth. Naturally, it also affects the breath.

*Everyone has heard of smokers'
breath. By not smoking you will
remove the cause and will
probably find that your lips are
in much greater demand.
Think about the irony of having
a shower, spraying yourself with
cologne or perfume and then
putting a cigarette in your
mouth and smoke in your
lungs as you walk out the door.*

Every day in the UK, 9,500 hospital beds are occupied by people who are suffering from diseases brought about by smoking.

You can do your bit for society by not smoking. Nurses are overworked and spend a lot of their working day caring for sick smokers. Don't be one. The Health Service could be a lot more effective if smokers would quit. Be an example of good health.

90% of peripheral vascular disease that leads to amputation develops from smoking.

When did you last ride a bicycle? Dig out your old bike, hire one or even buy one, and treat your legs and lungs to a work-out. You'll find it will help you to unwind, give you time to think and leave you feeling energised.

In Britain 40% of all cancer deaths are from lung cancer. It is rare in non-smokers.

Give yourself the best possible opportunities to live a full and problem-free life. To be alive is a gift that is often under-appreciated. Take the time to think about your life. How could you enjoy it more? How many times have you said, 'I'd love to…'? So do it. Try new things.

Britain loses at least 50 million working days each year due to sick leave brought about by smoking-related problems.

By claiming freedom from cigarettes you will increase your ability to perform well, to work better and to handle stress more easily. Not smoking will help you to be more successful in all areas of your life. Look forward to having more energy.

Smoking leads to a drop of around 30% in a woman's fertility. Furthermore, babies born to women who smoke are on average half a pound lighter than those born to mothers who do not smoke.

The countryside is a great calmer of thoughts. Stress and worries fade before its majesty. Find a green hillside or a view of the sea, and you will feel any worries you may have float away with every breath.

Each year more schoolchildren are starting to smoke. One survey found that by the age of 11 almost a quarter of British children had tried a cigarette.

Children will benefit from a good education, good health and a good example. Set a positive standard for the young. Encourage them to aspire to be happy and healthy.

**Male smokers often have a
lower sperm count, less
mobile sperm and
increased abnormalities
in sperm shape.**

Men, why not decide to be fit on the inside? We often concentrate on external keep fit, but the extremely important condition of our inner body is ignored. Drink more water and don't smoke. You'll feel a lot better for it.

Children whose parents smoke are more likely to develop cancer during their lifetime and are 30% more likely to develop glue ear, the commonest cause of childhood deafness.

*Think about what you would
like to teach your children,
nieces and nephews. Education
does not only come from
school. How you behave and
what you say and do are also
part of their lesson in life.*

It was estimated that in 1994, British children aged 11–16 spent £135 million on cigarettes. This provided £108 million to the government in tax revenue.

You probably feel you pay quite enough tax to the government. Ask yourself why cigarettes remain a legal drug despite the fact that they are well known to kill one in every two smokers.

Obstructive lung disease (emphysema) is a gradually developing condition which may become noticeable only after half of the lung has already been destroyed.

Pick a dream holiday destination. Visualise yourself walking along a beach and wading through warm blue waters. See if your local travel agent will let you pay weekly with the money you are saving from each week of not smoking.

Heavy smokers have 10–15 times more chance of dying from a heart attack before they reach the age of 45 than someone who does not smoke.

*You may already have, or want
to have, children. Resolve to be
around to see them marry, or
have their own children. By
claiming freedom from
cigarettes you will be putting
the odds of survival firmly in
your favour.*

It is estimated that as many as 12,000 cases of heart disease in the UK each year can be blamed on passive smoking.

It's odd how people cling to the idea of smoking to be 'sociable'. We must accept the fact that by smoking we may well fatally harm the very people we think we are being sociable with. Enjoy your friends and enjoy being sociable. Giving up cigarettes will benefit everyone you know, and everyone you care about.

Approximately one third of all pregnant women in the UK smoke. It has been estimated that every day one child dies in cot death because of the increased risks brought about by smoking.

*By not smoking, you will be
better able to finance your new
arrival with the money you are
saving. Giving up will go a long
way to buy all those fresh new
things you want and need for
your child.*

Once inhaled, smoke condenses, and about 70% of the tar in the smoke is deposited in the smoker's lung.

Discover cookery books. From the moment you stop smoking, your sense of taste will be improving, allowing you to explore a whole new world. Experiment with new flavours and foods. Learning to cook well improves the quality of every day.

Even smoking only one cigarette a day increases the chances of dying from lung cancer by 8 times.

Cutting down on the number of cigarettes you smoke is better than nothing, but nothing is better than not smoking at all. Decide to stop completely. That way the number cannot accidentally creep upwards.

17,000 children under 5 are admitted to hospital each year due to passive smoking.

*By choosing to stop smoking
you will be creating a much
healthier environment for your
children as they grow, and you
will be setting a good example
for them to reflect in their own
lives. That's something to be
proud of.*

Every year across Europe alone, more than half a million people die from smoking. It has been forecast that by the year 2030, based on current trends, 10 million people a year will be dying worldwide from smoking-related diseases.

Although this sounds like the number of casualties from a war, these deaths are brought about simply because of ignorance about the dangers of smoking. Share your knowledge and lead by example. When others see the improvements in your health after quitting, they'll want to do the same.

It is estimated that from every 1000 20-year-old smokers, 250 will die in mid-life from smoking.

Middle age is often the start of life, as it's then that we realise we are not merely passengers. You can choose your own direction. You can choose never to smoke another cigarette. Be responsible for your own health. Who else will be?

GPs give 8 million consultations each year dealing with smoking-related problems.

We would all like our country to excel in sports and international games. By having a population where a quarter of all adults smoke we promote a poor image to the young. By choosing to quit you will improve your own health immediately, and also pass on a better message to our new generations.

In the UK during 1997, single-parent families spent £365 million on cigarettes.

Sit down and work out exactly how much the habit of smoking costs you. Even add up the cost of lighter fuel or the matches that you use. Realise how smoking is holding you back financially. When you stop smoking, you will naturally have more cash available to put towards whatever is important to you.

One of the visible effects of smoking is the yellowing of the walls and ceilings of pubs. It is no surprise that smoking also stains fingers, hair and teeth.

The great news about stopping smoking is that the benefits begin straight away. Your body will start cleaning up as soon as you give it the chance. Check out the Good News section at the back of the book.

No one likes to be in a car or any other enclosed space with a smoker. Non-smokers often complain when coming home from a night out that their clothes 'stink of cigarettes'.

Once you have stopped smoking your clothes will lose the smell of stale smoke and you'll make a better impression on other people. Think of the new clothes that you will be able to afford by not spending your money on cigarettes. Have a treat day once a month and go out shopping.

In a survey 61% of pregnant smokers said that they received no advice on stopping smoking.

*Share information that you
have learned about smoking at
your pre-natal classes. Join up
with other smoking mothers
and quit together. If you can
stop smoking for 9 months, you
can stop for life.*

A smoker inhales only 15% of smoke from each cigarette. The other 85% drifts around him or her, and is inhaled by anyone nearby.

Being part of a group significantly increases your chances of quitting cigarettes. You will find a list of useful numbers in the back of this book. Alternatively talk to any of your friends who smoke and have a big joint effort to break the habit.

It has been estimated that a smoker loses one day from his or her life for each week of smoking.

Be aware of any routines that accompany your smoking habit. Think about when you smoke. If you always have a coffee and a cigarette after a meal, try avoiding the coffee and you may find that you ease the urge for a cigarette.

In advertisements looking for romance, flat-mates, employees or companions, non-smokers are often requested as a preference.

Remember, it is not the smoker who is unwelcome, but the smoking. By stopping the habit you may well find that you receive more invitations and opportunities. It is never a social problem to be a non-smoker.

Smoking kills one in two regular smokers. The same odds can be found by tossing a coin. No matter how long smoking lets you live, your life will be impaired by the habit. Heads you lose, tails you lose.

Be someone who stays around to be part of the family. You could consider pledging half of the money you will save from not smoking to a cause or charity that you feel strongly about.

**Smoking accounts for a fifth
of all UK deaths every year.**

*Replace an unhealthy pastime
with more healthy or interesting
ones. Take up an evening class
in something that has always
interested you. Don't worry
about it being of 'no real use'.
Indulge yourself. Change things.
Make your life more varied.*

Smoking-related diseases cost the NHS around £1.7 billion each year.

Go into your local bookstore and look in the self-help section. You'll find plenty of books on positive thinking and new ways to look at life. Lots of good advice is just waiting to be used. These books are not aimed at people with problems, but at people who want to get the most happiness and success out of life. Try some of them.

Smoking and the Environment

Besides the effect that smoking has on the smoker and the people nearby, it is worth remembering that cigarettes and their production have a direct and negative impact on the world environment.

Here are a few facts to consider.

• The tobacco plant has a three-month growth cycle, during which time up to 16 chemical applications are used. These chemicals seep into the soil, are carried by water and gradually enter the food chain.

• In Brazil alone, half a million acres of fertile land are used for tobacco crops.

• Huge areas of our planet are set aside to grow tobacco when the same land could be used to supply food, provide housing or sustain wildlife.

• Tobacco is the most heavily subsidised crop. The European Union spent £735 million in 1997 to subsidise tobacco growers.

• 200 trees are cut down every year to process the tobacco required for every 20-a-day smoker.

• Cigarette filters take up to two years to break down naturally.

• Every day British smokers throw away around 200 million cigarette butts and 20 million packets. Many of these end up on the ground and make up 40% of all items of street litter found in the UK.

The Good News

The good news is that from the moment that you stop smoking, your body begins the process of recovery. Although you may feel uncomfortable for the first few weeks, you can be sure that, inside your body, changes for the better are constantly taking place. Your life is getting better. Your body is getting fitter. You are becoming free from cigarettes.

Physical benefits from the moment of quitting
20 minutes
Your blood pressure and pulse rate normalise.

60 minutes
Your body starts to rid itself of tobacco toxins.

8 hours
Oxygen levels have returned to normal.
Carbon monoxide and nicotine levels in your blood have halved.

24 hours
Carbon monoxide is eliminated from your body.
Your lungs start clearing out mucus and smoking debris.

48 hours
Your senses of taste and smell have improved.
There is no nicotine left in your body.

72 hours
Your bronchial tubes have started to relax; breathing
becomes easier. You feel more alert.

2–12 weeks
Your general health is getting better.
Your ability to exercise improves.
There is better circulation around your body.

3–9 months
Your lung functioning is improved by 10–30%.
Any coughs, wheezing and breathing problems lessen.

10 months
Your lungs are cleared of tars.
Your energy levels are much improved.

5 years
Your risk of a heart attack drops to half that of a smoker.

10 years
Your risk of lung cancer falls to half that of a smoker.
Your risk of a heart attack falls to the same as someone
who has never smoked.

More Good News

As well as the physical good news for your body, freedom from cigarettes means personal good news too, for every aspect of your life.

Personal benefits from quitting
• You look healthier because your skin is better oxygenated.

• Your skin is clearer and will age more slowly.

• Your hair smells fresher.

• Your clothes smell fresh and clean.

• Your fingers and teeth have lost any nicotine staining.

• You enjoy feeling fitter.

• You can sit anywhere you want to in a restaurant.

• Your home and car have lost the smell of cigarettes.

• You have made a positive choice about your life.

- You feel proud of your accomplishment.

- You can cope more easily with exertion.

- You are setting a good example.

- You have removed the risk of being harmful to those close to you.

- You no longer feel stressed about the dangers of smoking.

- You feel better about yourself.

- You have more money.

- Your children are safer.

- You perform better at any physical activity.

- Your breath does not carry the smell of stale smoke.

- You get more out of life.

- You will live longer and be healthier.

- You are free.

Help

You may find it helpful to join forces with friends, colleagues or members of your family who also want to quit. In a shared effort to stop smoking you will benefit from mutual support and encouragement. It will also be an added advantage if your friends are no longer smoking around you.

Workshops and meetings to help those who want to give up smoking are held regularly in all regions of the UK. It has been found that joining a group or a smoking clinic improves the success rate of quitting by up to four times. Call the numbers listed for details of your nearest groups. Or ask your doctor or at your local health centre.

The following regional helplines give information and advice aimed at helping you to stop smoking.

Quitline – England	0800 00 22 00
Smokeline – Scotland	0800 84 84 84
Wales	0345 69 75 00
Northern Ireland	01232 66 32 81

The Department of Health also has a helpline – 0800 169 0169

There is a wealth of books and information available covering the effects of smoking and different methods of quitting. The facts and statistics quoted in this book will be found validated at many sources. The Internet provides an enormous amount of detailed information and help. Should you wish to explore this facility, the following excellent websites make a very good starting point:

www.ash.org.uk
www.healthnet.org.uk
www.lifesaver.co.uk
www.givingupsmoking.co.uk

There is also a new monthly magazine aimed solely at smokers who want to quit. *STOP!* magazine can be found at branches of Boots, Superdrug and W. H. Smith. Alternatively, contact:

STOP! Magazine Ltd
70C High St
Whitstable
Kent
CT5 1BB
Tel: 01227 779 229

What's the alternative?

The best way to quit smoking is the one that works best for *you*. Some people manage simply to stub out their cigarette and never light another. Others prefer to use nicotine replacement therapy (NRT) in the form of patches, lozenges, gum, etc. to help them. This method gives measured doses of nicotine while you break free from the smoking habit, and has proved itself to be very effective. Talk to your doctor or chemist to discuss the best method and dosage for you.

As smoking affects the whole body and can dominate all aspects of a smoker's life, some smokers find it helpful to turn to holistic or alternative therapies, which work on many levels of the body and mind. Some of these are used with great success, in particular acupuncture and hypnosis.

Further information and details of qualified practitioners in your area can be found at the following addresses. Please enclose an SAE.

Acupuncture
The British Acupuncture Council
63 Jeddo Road, London W12 9HQ
Tel: 020 8735 0400

Hypnosis
British Hypnotherapy Association
For a list of local registered therapists, freephone 0800 731 8443

When giving up smoking you may feel more on edge than usual. This will usually pass after a couple of weeks, but to restore a sense of calm and also to aid the breakdown of toxins, it may help to book yourself in for a massage. An aromatherapy massage is particularly relaxing, as is reflexology (foot massage). Try these therapies. The simple joys of relaxation and quiet bliss are strangely undervalued in our busy world.

To find your nearest practitioner, contact:

The British Register of Complementary Practitioners
PO Box 194, London SE16 7QZ (sae with two first-class stamps)
Tel: 020 7237 5165

Association of Reflexologists
27 Old Gloucester Street
London WC1N 3XX (A5 sae with 40p stamp)
Tel: 09906 73320

The Day I Stopped Smoking

Date _____

Signature _____

Reasons Why I Am Not Going to Smoke

_____

_____

_____

_____

_____

_____

_____

Signature _____

The Amount of Money I Usually Spend on Smoking

_____

_____

_____

_____

_____

_____

_____

_____

My Rewards for Quitting

1 day _____

3 days _____

1 week _____

2 weeks _____

1 month _____

2 months _____

3 months _____

6 months _____

1 year _____

Notes

_____

_____

_____

_____

_____

_____

_____

_____

_____